Rainforests

By John Wood

BookLife

©2018
Book Life
King's Lynn
Norfolk PE30 4LS

ISBN: 978-1-78637-130-0 ·

Written by:
John Wood

Edited by:
Holly Duhig

Designed by:
Matt Rumbelow

A catalogue record for this book
is available from the British Library.

Photocredits: Abbreviations: l-left, r-right, b-bottom, t-top, c-centre, m-middle. Images are courtesy of Shutterstock.com. With thanks to Getty Images, Thinkstock Photo and iStockphoto. 2 - Curioso. 3 - Twinsterphoto. 4 - MarcusVDT. 5: tl - Daniel Etzold; mc - Dudarev Mikhail; mr - Zephyr_p; bl - Ilyshev Dmitry; br - Piotr Krzeslak. 6 - Galyna Andrushko. 7 - Ammit Jack. 8 - Gustavo Frazao. 9: tl - Kjersti Joergensen; mr - fototrips; bl - Dr Morley Read. 10 - RAJU SONI. 11 - dangdumrong. 12 - Dr Morley Read. 13 - khlungcenter. 14 - Sharp. 15 - Vladimir Wrangel. 16 - Michael Lynch. 17 - belizar. 18 - Ryan M. Bolton. 19 -Vladimir Wrangel. 20 - Rich Carey. 21 - Rich Carey. 22 - Sergey Uryadnikov. 23 - reptiles4all.

CONTENTS

Page 4   What Is a Habitat?

Page 6   What Is a Rainforest?

Page 8   Types of Rainforest Habitat

Page 10   Bengal Tigers

Page 12   Leaf Cutter Ants

Page 14   Sloths

Page 16   Vampire Bats

Page 18   Green Anacondas

Page 20   Rainforests in Danger

Page 22   Endangered Animals

Page 24   Glossary and Index

Words that look like this can be found in the glossary on page 24.

WHAT IS A
HABITAT?

A habitat is a place where an animal lives. It provides the animal with food, shelter and everything else it needs to survive.

There are lots of different habitats in the world. Each one is home to many different animals.

Mountains

Oceans

The Arctic

Deserts

Forests

5

WHAT IS A RAINFOREST?

A rainforest is another word for a jungle. Rainforests grow in hot countries near the equator, where it rains a lot. This means the weather is wet and warm.

Rainforest

The biggest rainforest in the world is the Amazon rainforest in South America. It is home to lots of plants and animals that aren't found anywhere else in the world.

The Amazon Rainforest

The Amazon

South America

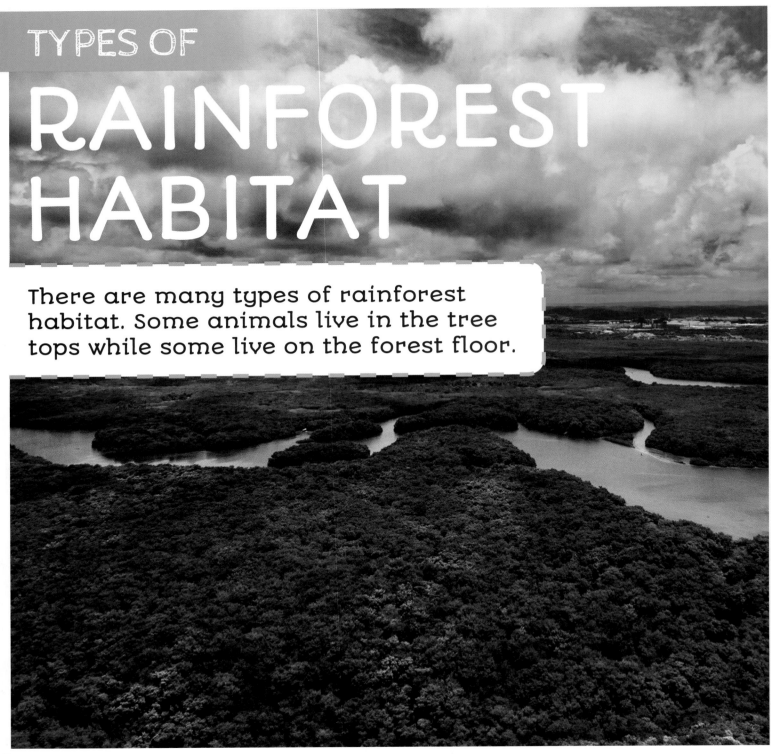

RAINFOREST HABITAT

There are many types of rainforest habitat. Some animals live in the tree tops while some live on the forest floor.

Other animals live in the thick layer of trees called the rainforest canopy. Rivers that run through rainforests also provide a habitat for many animals.

Treetops

Rainforest Canopy

Forest Floor

BENGAL TIGERS

Bengal tigers are one of the biggest animals in the rainforest. They live on the forest floor. When hunting their prey, tigers hide among small plants.

Tigers like to make the whole rainforest their home. They roam around, climbing trees and swimming in rivers.

Every tiger has a different pattern of stripes.

LEAF-CUTTER ANTS

Leaf-cutter ants live in nests underground in a big group called a colony. There can be over one million ants in a single colony.

The ants carry leaves from rainforest trees back to their home under the forest floor. Fungus grows on the leaves which the ants eat later.

SLOTHS

One of the many animals that live in the rainforest canopy is the sloth. Sloths spend most of their lives hanging in trees and moving very slowly.

Sloth

Sometimes, small insects and algae live and grow in the sloth's fur. This makes the sloth look green, which helps them to hide from predators in the green canopy.

VAMPIRE BATS

Vampire bats live high up in the treetops. When they aren't flying, bats usually hang upside down.

Bats sleep during the day and hunt at night.

They hunt by sneaking up on sleeping animals and drinking a small amount of their blood. Most of the time, the animals don't even wake up.

GREEN ANACONDAS

Green anacondas are the heaviest snakes in the world. They spend most of their time in rivers and swamps, where they can move quickly.

The Anaconda's scales make it hard for them to be seen in the water. Anacondas quietly wait for animals to come near the water before they attack.

RAINFORESTS IN
DANGER

People cut down rainforest trees to make room for roads and buildings. They also use the wood to make things like paper and furniture. When lots of trees get cut down, it is called deforestation.

Deforestation destroys many animal homes, which makes it hard for them to survive. When animals find it hard to survive, they are said to be endangered.

ORANGUTANS

As large areas of rainforest are chopped down, orangutans have fewer trees to live and find food in. This can cause orangutans to starve.

POISON DART FROGS

Some types of poison dart frogs are endangered. These frogs eat insects on the forest floor, but people are using this space to build farms and buildings.

GLOSSARY

algae	living things that are like plants, but have no roots, stems, leaves or flowers
colony	a nest where ants live together, which is usually underground
endangered	when a species of animal is in danger of going extinct
equator	the imaginary line around the Earth that is an equal distance from the North and South Poles
predators	animals that hunt other animals for food
prey	animals that are hunted by other animals for food
roam	wander freely or aimlessly, often over a wide area
scales	small circles of thin bone that protect the skin of fish and reptiles
shelter	protection from danger and harsh weather
starve	when something dies because it doesn't eat enough food

Index

canopy 9, 14, 15
forest floor 8-10 13, 23
hiding 10, 15
hunting 10, 16-17
insects 15, 23

predators 15
prey 10
rivers 9, 11, 18
sleeping 16-17
trees 8-9, 11, 13-14, 16, 20, 22